STAFF DEVELOPMENT VIDEO

THE ART OF TEACHING ESL

PARTICIPANT'S GUIDE

▲▼ Addison-Wesley Publishing Company
Reading, Massachusetts • Menlo Park, California • New York • Don Mills, Ontario • Wokingham, England
Amsterdam • Bonn • Sydney • Singapore • Tokyo • Madrid • San Juan

Project Director:	Judith Bittinger
Editorial Development:	Jeanine Ardourel, Evelyn Nelson, Karen Doyle
Cover Design:	Marshall Henrichs
Production/Manufacturing:	James W. Gibbons
Video Shoot and Production:	Cheryl McElvain, Judith Bittinger, Penrose Productions, Menlo Park, California

Video Musical Credits

Opening and closing music from *One Big Family* by Bob Schneider. © 1986 by Schorn Publishing. All rights reserved.

Students singing from *In a Child's Heart* by Bob Schneider. © 1986 by Schorn Publishing. All rights reserved.

Students singing from *The Salt and Pepper Shake* by Bob Schneider. © 1989 by Schorn Publishing. All rights reserved.

Some material adapted from the Addison-Wesley program *TLLC (Teaching Language, Literature, and Culture)* by McCloskey, Hooper, and Linse as well as from other Addison-Wesley publications for teachers.

The Cognitive Academic Language Learning Approach (CALLA), described on pages 49–59, was created by Anna Uhl Chamot and J. Michael O'Malley and is featured in several Addison-Wesley publications.

The Art of Teaching ESL video is protected electronically. Attempts to copy may damage the video.

Copyright © 1993 by Addison-Wesley Publishing Company, Inc.
All rights reserved. No part of this publication may be reproduced, stored in a retrieval system, or transmitted in any form or by any means, electronic, mechanical, photocopying, recording, or otherwise, without the prior written permission of the publisher. Printed in the United States of America.

ISBN 0-201-50171-6
3 4 5 6 7 8 9 10-CRS-00999897

The Art of Teaching ESL was filmed at the Curtner School in Milpitas, California. We would like to thank the teachers and students who participated in this program for their enthusiasm and good will.

We would also like to acknowledge the following talented and committed educators who contributed greatly to this program: Cheryl McElvain, ELD Resource Specialist, Milpitas Unified School District, Milpitas, California; Teresa Walter, Resource Teacher/ESL Trainer, San Diego Unified School District, San Diego, California; Allene Guss Grognet, Vice-President, Center for Applied Linguistics, Sarasota, Florida; Phyllis Ziegler, ESL/Bilingual Consultant, New York, New York; Heather Sellens, ESL Consultant/LDS Trainer, Elk Grove, California.

Contents

Strategies Checklist Chart vii

Introduction ix

Part 1: Effective Teaching Strategies and Learning Environments 1

    The Basics of Teaching Limited English Proficient Students   1
    Cooperative Learning   9
    Process Writing   13
    Content-Area Instruction   17
    The Role of Literature   22

Part 2: Approaches and Techniques: Video Segments and Activities 24

    Total Physical Response - TPR   24
        (*The Alphabet Cheer*)
    The Natural Approach   28
        (*The Meal*)
    The Language Experience Approach   33
        (*Naughty Marisia*)
    Integrated Language Teaching   38
        (*Poems about Feelings*)
    Whole Language/Whole Language Assessment   42
        (*The Farmer and the Beet*)
    The Cognitive, Academic Language Learning Approach - CALLA   49
        (*Light and Shadow*)
    The Functional-Notional Approach to Syllabus Design   53
        (*no video segment*)
    The Structural Approach to Syllabus Design   54
        (*no video segment*)

Part 3: Culminating Video Segments and Activities 55

    Tip Top Adventures   56
    Shape People/Kachina Dolls   59
    The Salt and Pepper Shake   62

Bibliography 67

Strategies Checklist Chart

This chart lists each video segment featured in Parts 2 and 3 of *The Art of Teaching ESL* videotape and the strategies and approaches that are central to this staff development program. Each video segment illustrates a number of the strategies through a classroom lesson. The segments are listed in the order in which they appear on the videotape, along with the page numbers in this guide on which the lessons are discussed.

To find a specific lesson on the tape, simply fast forward to the title of the lesson.

As you complete a lesson, return to this chart and check off the strategies and/or approaches you explored.

Video Segments	Cooperative Learning	Process Writing	Content-area Instruction	Literature	TPR	Natural Approach	Language Experience Approach	Integrated Language Teaching	Whole Language	CALLA
Part 2										
Alphabet Cheer										
pp. 26–27										
The Meal										
pp. 30–32										
Naughty Marisia										
pp. 36–37										
Poems About Feelings										
pp. 40–41										
The Farmer and the Beet										
pp. 45–46										
Light and Shadow										
pp. 51–52										
Part 3										
Tip Top Adventures										
pp. 56–58										
ShapePeople/ Kachina Dolls										
pp. 59–61										
The Salt and Pepper Shake										
pp. 62–64										

Introduction

Welcome!

The purpose of *The Art of Teaching ESL* staff development program is to help you put the latest instructional ideas and methods in second language teaching into practice with confidence and ease. The strategies and approaches explored in this guide and on the video may be used in a variety of situations—in a standard, self-contained classroom that includes LEP students, in an ESL pull-out class, in a sheltered English class, or in a bilingual class. Whether you are an experienced teacher or a neophyte, this program can raise the level of your professional skills and the level of personal satisfaction you feel from a job well done. Like an artist, you will use the techniques and tools of your trade to widen, redefine, and refine your own teaching style and creative powers as you explore *The Art of Teaching ESL*.

The examples on the video are from *Teaching Language, Literature, and Culture* and the *Addison-Wesley ESL* program. The video lessons take place in mainstream classrooms and in one pull-out ESL class. You will see how English-only students and limited-English-speaking students respond in different ways to a lesson and make the language experience uniquely their own.

Organization of the Guide

This guide is your personal journal and record of staff development sessions. It is organized into three parts. Part 1 covers the basics of teaching LEP students, describes the philosophical background and theoretical rationale of strategies that can be used with approaches to language instruction, and provides practical instructions on how to set up effective learning environments. Each section of Part 2 describes a specific language teaching approach or technique, its philosophical background, and basic steps of implementation. The video segment that follows shows the approach in action. *Pre-view Notes* encourage critical viewing. *Post-view Discussion* questions are explored in small groups. In *Application Activities* teachers work cooperatively in small groups to develop new lessons that use the approach presented.

In Part 3, the video segments show how instructional strategies and approaches are interwoven and combined. Here teachers "put it all together" in culminating activities that show proof of understanding.

Workshop leaders can use this flexible format to schedule staff development to meet their needs—from one-hour sessions to a full day or longer.

PART 1: Effective Teaching Strategies and Learning Environments

The Basics of Teaching Limited English Proficient Students

The following teaching strategies are effective for all students but are especially powerful for limited English proficient (LEP) students. When making instructional decisions about grouping and activities, select and integrate these techniques where they will provide the LEP student with maximum access to learning.

Communicating with your ESL students

- Use gestures, facial expression, emphasis, and pantomime to help communicate the meaning of your words. These nonverbal communication techniques help even very beginning English learners understand what is going on.

- Use pictures, props, and real objects to introduce vocabulary and ideas. Children learn through concrete experiences. Provide children with lots of opportunities to practice and explore language and ideas through manipulative materials and creative play.

- Use charts, graphs, and manipulatives to present and explore concepts and language.

- Repeat, recycle, and rephrase key language "chunks." Using the same or similar phrases in a variety of contexts helps students develop vocabulary and language usage concepts. Help students to adapt the language patterns in predictable songs, poems, and stories, and to create their own verses and stories.

- Use both adults and peers to model language. Present children with a variety of English-speaking voices. Invite family and community members into your class to tell stories, teach songs, read books, and share experiences. Record your students as they recite familiar rhymes or participate in shared readings. Parents and other family members can tape record themselves reading predictable books students know and like. All these tape recordings can be placed in the Listening Center for students to enjoy independently, often with a copy of the book or poem chart.

- Respect "the silent period" during which beginning language learners are often hesitant to speak. TPR activities, repetitious, predictable stories and songs, and concrete, hands-on activities allow children at all language levels to participate in a learning experience.

- Offer students a variety of ways to respond in activities. Respect individual learning styles and preferences and accommodate different levels of language skill.

- Find opportunities for one-on-one sharing. Individual interactions with children have many advantages. You can tailor your language to the child's level. The child is often more comfortable speaking to only one person. Small group work and independent learning center activities provide times when the teacher can "float" and attend to individuals.

- Establish a comfortable atmosphere in your classroom: one that values, encourages, and celebrates students' efforts to use language. Focus on and respond to the ideas being communicated, rather than "errors" in the language forms.

- Give students back their own language with elaborations and modifications. As you talk with young language learners, listen carefully for what they are trying to say and repeat their ideas back to them, rephrasing and asking them for clarification or confirmation. Rather than directly correcting students' language, model correct terms and forms and elaborate on their language in your natural conversation with them.

- Focus on students' previous knowledge and vocabulary.

- Draw on past experiences of your students as those experiences relate to the theme of the lesson. Concepts learned in any language will transfer to English.

Language Development Activities

Listening

- Have students view movies and tapes related to the targeted theme.
- Read aloud to students every day.

- Provide auditory identification activities that relate to a theme. For example, for the theme "sounds," have students close their eyes and identify different sounds, such as a door being closed, a book being shut, using chalk to write on the board.
- Have students listen to a story on tape and then sequence pictures according to the order of events in the story.
- Read, or provide tapes of, various pieces of extended literature appropriate to students' interests, ages, and proficiency levels.
- Provide opportunities for students to listen to several versions of the same story and discuss similarities and differences of the versions.
- Have students play "pictionary," in which they draw pictures as clues for their team members to guess a word or phrase (such as a book title) that has been provided by an opposing team.

Speaking

- Encourage students to discuss and describe personal experiences that relate to a theme. Don't force production, however.
- Encourage students to describe pictures.
- Expand concepts and vocabulary through role-play.
- Have students read a story and then retell it orally.
- Have students predict story plot developments or endings.
- Have students memorize and recite in unison poems related to a theme.
- Provide reader's theater scripts for class "productions" of stories.
- Provide opportunities for students to interview teachers, parents, and other students.
- Have students dramatize readings or current event articles.
- Encourage students to compare and contrast vocabulary using synonyms, homonyms, and antonyms, for example.

Reading

- Engage students in shared reading activities.
- Use comic strips for teaching sequence and reinforcing comprehension.
- Play word games with antonyms, synonyms, and homonyms.
- Read riddles and simple jokes.

- Read and discuss idioms.
- Read other students' writing.
- Provide and encourage students to use a reading corner that is stocked with high interest, low readability books.
- Encourage students to read books written in their primary language.

Writing
- Use language experience stories that are thematic.
- Have students brainstorm ideas on paper.
- Allow developmental spelling. Focus on fluency rather than form.
- Encourage students to use the word-cluster technique for brainstorming.
- Use word banks.
- Develop individual student dictionaries.
- Develop character and story maps.
- Categorize vocabulary.
- Develop sensory word lists.
- Use concrete poetry and onomatopoeia.
- Use pattern book writing units that relate to a theme.
- Be sure that grammar corrections are contextual.
- Provide frequent opportunities for journal writing.
- Provide dictation.

Setting up a Learning Center

A Learning Center can be as simple as a collection of materials in a bin on a table, or a well-established area in the classroom including display boards, tables, and shelves.

Learning Centers provide wonderful opportunities for children to explore materials, ideas, and language independently and/or with classmates. The child-directed learning that takes place in Learning Centers is an important complement to teacher-directed instruction and activities. At Learning Centers, students are encouraged to experiment and consult with peers, instead of relying on teacher expertise. They gain skill and confidence as independent learners.

Labeling Learning Center materials

It is important to label materials with print and pictures, and clearly indicate where each type of material is to be stored. Labeling reinforces children's awareness of the value of print in their environment and helps them make connections between print and the materials they are using. It also fosters independence as children begin to assume responsibility for finding the materials they want to use and then returning them to their proper place.

Using rebus directions at Learning Centers

Rebus or picture directions offer another meaningful way to incorporate print in a Learning Center and help facilitate self-directed, independent learning. Visual clues provide comprehensible input.

How many children can use a Learning Center at a given time?

Different Learning Centers can be designed to accommodate different numbers of students. Consider the amount of space each child will need for the activity, the level of supervision required, and the cooperative atmosphere you hope to establish at the Center. If you are limiting the number of children that can participate in a given center at one time, provide concrete cues to help students remember and abide by this limit. For example, the number of chairs at a table can stipulate the number of students allowed at that center at one time. A set number of armbands, hats, necklaces, etc. can be provided for students to wear while working in a Center. A rebus sign with a number and a sketch of that many children is another way of reminding children of the limit.

Capitalizing on students' interest

If Matrioska stacking dolls are a popular attraction in the Math Center, try placing similar sets of stacking dolls in the Art Center or the Drama Center. Provide envelopes and boxes in the Art Center so children can create their own stacking "doll" sets. Students will be encouraged to devise new ways to use familiar toys.

Establishing a Multicultural Classroom

> Multicultural education is not a set curriculum, but a perspective that is reflected in all decisions about every phase and aspect of teaching. It is a lens through which teachers can scrutinize their options and choices in order to clarify what social information they are conveying overtly and covertly to their students. (Ramsey, 1987)

A meaningful approach to multicultural education is based on respect for and appreciation of individual, family, and cultural diversity. For young children, meaningful multicultural awareness grows from concrete, positive personal experiences. As children work, play, and talk together they learn from each other and celebrate the diversity within the class and the community.

If students in your class come from family cultures that are quite different then your native culture, you will need to find out more about the children's cultures. Your best resources for information are the children and their parents. Community organizations representing different cultural groups, colleagues who share a cultural background with the children or have learned from them over the years, and books are other good sources.

To be a student of culture you need to be patient and observant. Suspend judgment and be aware of your own cultural bias in interpreting students' behavior. Behavioral standards are not universal. What is common and expected in one culture may be unacceptable in another. Students who consistently "interrupt" conversations or hesitate to chime in may be reflecting behavioral norms supported by their home cultures. Body language or nonverbal communication is also culturally based. In some cultures, avoiding eye contact is interpreted as evasiveness or apathy; in other cultures, focusing your eyes downwards is seen as a sign of respect. Sensitivity, respect, and increasing knowledge of different cultural expectations will help you gain understanding of your students and their families.

You also need an understanding of the difference between deep culture and surface culture. Elements of surface culture are more easily identified and celebrated then the elements of deep culture.

Elements of Surface Culture

1. FOOD: food and culinary contributions

2. HOLIDAYS: patriotic holidays, religious observances, and personal rites and celebrations

3. ARTS: traditional and contemporary music, visual and performing arts, and drama

4. FOLKLORE: folk tales, legends, and oral history

5. HISTORY: historical and humanitarian contributions and social and political movements

6. PERSONALITIES: historical, contemporary, and local figures

Elements of Deep Culture

1. CEREMONY: what a person is to say and do on particular occasions

2. COURTSHIP & MARRIAGE: attitudes toward dating, marriage, and raising a family

3. ESTHETICS: the beautiful things of culture: literature, music, dance, art, architecture, and how they are enjoyed

4. ETHICS: how a person learns and practices honesty, fair play, principles, moral thought, etc.

5. FAMILY TIES: how a person feels towards his or her family and friends.

6. HEALTH & MEDICINE: how a person reacts to sickness, death, soundness of mind and body, medicine, etc.

7. FOLK MYTHS: attitudes toward heroes, traditional stories, legendary characters, superstitions, etc.

8. GESTURE & KINESTHETICS: forms of nonverbal communication of reinforced speech, such as the use of the eyes, the hands, and the body

9. GROOMING & PRESENCE: the cultural differences in personal behavior and appearance, such as laughter, smile, voice quality, gait, poise, hair style, cosmetics, dress, etc.

10. OWNERSHIP: attitudes toward ownership of property, individual rights, loyalties, beliefs, etc.

11. PRECEDENCE: what are accepted manners toward older persons, peers, younger persons

12. REWARDS & PRIVILEGE: attitudes toward motivation, merit, achievement, service, social position, etc.

13. RIGHTS & DUTIES: attitudes toward personal obligations, voting, taxes, military service, legal rights, personal demands, etc.

14. RELIGION: attitudes toward the divine and the supernatural and how they affect a person's thoughts and actions

15. SEX ROLES: how a person views, understands, and relates to members of the opposite sex and what deviations are allowed and expected

16. SPACE & PROXEMICS: attitudes toward self and land; the accepted distances between individuals within a culture

17. SUBSISTENCE: attitudes about providing for oneself, the young, and the old, and who protects whom

18. TABOOS: attitudes and beliefs about doing things against culturally accepted patterns

19. CONCEPTS OF TIME: attitudes toward being early, on time, or late

20. VALUES: attitudes toward freedom, education, cleanliness, cruelty, crime, etc.

From: Gonzales, Frank. Mexican American Culture in the Bilingual Education Classroom. Unpublished doctoral dissertation, The University of Texas at Austin, 1978.

Remember . . .

To ensure success:

- Remain open and patient; understanding another culture is a continuous and not a discrete process.

- Integrate students' life experiences with new school activities and learning.

- Utilize dramatic play, art, music, and stories that reflect topics central to children's lives—mealtime and bedtime ritual, cultural holidays, etc.

- Fill your classroom with toys, books, pictures, and props that include images of people that look like the children and that affirm their cultural life styles.

- Expand the notion that students should learn about cultures not necessarily represented in their own classroom. This should be part of an overall school philosophy.

Cooperative Learning

Background

> We cannot . . . afford to have a significant number of students who are alienated, left out, disconnected from their peers. We cannot afford to graduate large numbers of students with little or no ability to interact effectively with others—a prime requisite in the world of work. And we cannot afford to teach students in an environment where they will not learn as much as they could. (Johnson, Johnson, Holubec & Roy, 1984)

Cooperative learning with peers is extremely important and valuable for young children. Organizing classroom interactions to incorporate cooperative learning improves academic achievement, encourages better relations among students of different backgrounds, and results in better attitudes towards school, learning, and self. When small groups of students collaborate on a common task, they must clarify and negotiate meaning with one another. This exchange of information and ideas provides rich language learning opportunities for young ESL students.

The cooperative learning environment offers many other rewards. Learners become more active, self-directed, and communicative. Discipline often improves because children are interested in what they are doing. Teachers have more time to work with small groups and individuals. Many ESL students come from home cultures where cooperation, sharing, and group achievement are highly valued. A cooperative classroom is a particularly affirming environment for these children.

> Students who learn to work with each other in cooperative learning groups based on mutual interest and criteria other than ability develop their capacity to use language creatively and critically. They also demonstrate higher academic performance, more positive attitudes toward school and learning, and better ethnic and cultural understanding and relations. (California State Department of Education, 1987)

Most activities and assignments that students participate in individually can be easily adapted to a cooperative learning format. It is the manner in which the materials are used, not the materials themselves, that enables students to work effectively in groups. The following techniques allow you to adapt any lesson for cooperative learning.

Heterogeneous Groups

- Set up heterogeneous groups of four to five students. When selecting groupings, maintain an even boy/girl ratio and try to avoid grouping best friends or enemies. Also attempt to make groups heterogeneous in terms of capacity for leadership, ethnology, citizenship, and attendance records.

- Post group lists or write them on the chalkboard.
- Establish rules for working in groups: move into groups quietly, work with quiet voices, stay with group, everyone should participate, everyone should use good social skills.

Room Arrangement

- Permanent arrangement: Desks are placed together throughout the day. Students may stay in their groups all day, or they may move in and out of their cooperative learning areas as necessary.
- Temporary arrangement: Students move their desks into groups during cooperative learning activities. Stage a practice drill when groups are first formed so that the process of moving desks becomes automatic.

Social Skills

- Create a list of social skills with your students (for example: *make eye contact with others when listening or speaking, make positive comments, give compliments, listen to others, assist others, share ideas and materials, take turns*). Tell students that they will use all these skills when working in cooperative groups.
- Discuss with students the meaning of each social skill. Elicit why each is important.
- Role-play with students to demonstrate each social skill.
- Emphasize social skills throughout the day, not just during cooperative learning.
- Concentrate on one or two skills at a time.
- Post a social skills chart.
- Debrief students on their use of social skills at the end of a lesson. Students might assess themselves individually (*I shared in my group, listened to others, used eye contact, used good manners, gave compliments, took turns*). Groups might assess themselves (*We contributed ideas, asked others for ideas, summarized information, listened to others with care, included everyone, made sure everyone understood*).

Team Members' Roles and Assignments

- Make teams aware of roles for group members. Roles can be combined or adapted for smaller groups.

   Encourager: in charge of manners and positive comments; gently reminds others to be positive

Participation monitor: makes sure that everyone listens and shares; energizes the group when motivation is low

Noise monitor: gently reminds team members to whisper or to keep noise within voice level

Director: organizes the group and develops the plan of action (what shall we do first, second. . . ?); makes sure everyone takes turns

Reviewer: goes over the plan of action to determine if and how the group accomplished goals; reports to the class

- Within two weeks of group formation, have groups decide which team members are best suited for each role.

Cooperative Learning during Teacher-Directed Instruction

- Check for understanding with partners: Instead of asking individual students questions to check understanding of the skill you are teaching, ask questions and have students turn to a neighbor and tell him or her the answer. This method allows more students to participate in responding to questions.

- Check for understanding with groups: Have each cooperative learning group decide on an answer to your question. The group's spokesperson can give a single answer to the class.

- Structured practice: When teaching a new skill, give a problem and tell each group to work it out together, making sure that all members understand the process.

- Problem solving, critical thinking, brainstorming: Ask an open-ended question and see how many alternative solutions each group can think of.

Cooperative Learning during Pair Practice

- Instead of having each student complete a worksheet individually, have two students work together, with one student completing even-numbered exercises and the other odd-numbered. Students could use pens or crayons of different colors to differentiate answers.

- After completing worksheets individually, pairs can compare answers and discuss answers they differ on.

- Students can help each other practice skills and concepts involving memory by taking turns quizzing each other from flashcards.

Cooperative Learning during Homework

- **Group rewards:** Give five bonus points to groups in which all members turn in their homework. Let the groups check their answers and work together before turning in their papers.

- Have each group compare answers and turn in just one group answer sheet, with individual homework sheets stapled to the back of the group sheet.

Remember . . .

To ensure success:

- Choose cooperative games in which there are no losers.

- Reinforce the use of social skills throughout the day, not just during cooperative learning activities.

- Model giving compliments at every opportunity. Write notes to students and their parents; recognize all group efforts.

- Allow students (at least some of the time) to choose their own groups.

- Set up groups that represent a cross-section of the class in terms of sex, ethnic background, and language level. This allows children access to an enriching variety of language, cultural, and cognitive input.

- Use Learning Centers; here students socialize, chat, ask for help, and exchange ideas as they collaborate.

Process Writing

Children need time to be children, to grow through natural childhood activities. It is not children—but adults—who have separated writing from art, song, and play; it is adults who have turned writing into an exercise on dotted-line paper, into a matter of rules, lessons, and cautious behavior. Children view writing quite differently. For them, it is exploration with marker and pen. Long before they come to school, youngsters leave their mark on foggy car windows and wet benches. (Calkins, 1986)

Background

Process writing is a strategy that professional writers use. Over the years, process writing has been used effectively with students who speak English as a second language, as well as with native English speakers.

The writing process for second language students should take place in an environment that is full of print, where students can collaborate and support each other as writers and where there are opportunities for students to create meaningful discourse in writing. (Enright and McCloskey, 1988)

Children practice authorship as they dictate language experience stories and create new verses and stories reusing predictable story language and story patterns. They also do their own "scribing," exploring what they know about the language, letters and sounds, and conventions of print as they write. As they experiment, they make discoveries and their writing changes and develops.

Teachers must be genuinely interested in what students have to say. Students' attempts to write and to progress in writing—from scribbling, to drawing, to making writing-like marks, to invented spelling, to conventional spelling—are celebrated, and "mistakes" are seen as a natural part of the development process. Just as we are thrilled with a baby's first attempts at speech, we should be delighted by a child's first attempts to write. Whether or not children are in a bilingual program, their attempts at writing in native languages are also encouraged and celebrated as part of their developing literacy.

Fill the classroom with opportunities and reasons to read and write. Interesting charts, books, posters, and student work are displayed and accessible to the students. Environmental print—such as labels from familiar products and authentic signs (*Exit, Stop, Listening Center*)—is also displayed. Students are read to and participate in reading and authoring events daily. Students' work is published, admired, and discussed. Books, authors, and writing are frequent topics of discussion.

The process consists of six stages: prewriting, drafting, sharing and responding to writing, revision, editing, and publishing or presenting. Your ESL activities may include all six stages, or only one or two of the process.

Adapt these steps to suit the needs of individual students and different writing situations. For example, most young children and inexperienced writers are not interested in revising their work. For these students, omit or modify that step. In real life and in the classroom, many types of writing are complete after the first draft. Only selected pieces are developed through all the steps.

Step 1 Prewriting

Prewriting experiences help students develop the need and desire to write. They involve students in motivating experiences and help them collect a resource pool of possible writing ideas, vocabulary, syntax, and language structures.

Encourage students to use prewriting as the basis for a wide variety of written pieces, including recipes, food can labels, song verses, short stories, advertisements, book reports, essays, letters, and thank-you notes.

As a teacher working with ESL students, you will find that it is often helpful to spend additional time on the prewriting stage of the process. Students may need additional time to work out orally what they would like to write. In addition, when you work with students from different cultural groups, be sure to encourage them to celebrate their cultural heritage by writing about their experiences. Give writing assignments in such a way that the children can describe what is meaningful to them.

Step 2 Drafting

At this point the student only works to get ideas down on paper. There is no concern about spelling and punctuation, but there is a desire to share ideas and to retain the flow of those ideas.

Children may scribble, draw, make letter-like marks on the page, arrange letters in a way that looks random on the page, or use "invented spelling." Encourage your young writers to make their best guesses about what writing should look like or how to spell a word. Encourage them at each stage of their writing and celebrate what their writing shows they *do* know.

Step 3 Sharing and Responding to Writing

Students confer with the teacher and share writing in pairs or small and large groups to get comments and to receive feedback about the content.

At this stage students work on refining, expanding, and elaborating on what they have written. The focus should be on content and not on grammar or punctuation, unless those errors obscure the meaning. Although young language learners may not be actually "reading" standard writing in the conversational sense when they share their works with you and/or classmates, they are learning to remember and tell stories, and to use pictures and symbolic cues to help them remember. You may wish to designate a special "author's chair" where, several times a week, students can sit and share their literary work with the group. Help students learn how to respond to their classmates' writing in supportive ways by modeling positive responses and thoughtful questions: "I really like the way you used the word *freckle*." "The part where the turtle turned into a monster was scary!" "Why did your grandmother say that?" "What did the dog look like?"

Step 4 Revising

Next, students revise their writing in order to make it clearer or, perhaps, to change the content. This is the time when polish is added to particular pieces of writing.

If children are not ready for revision, you can begin to model this step and have them help you revise. This works particularly well with group language experience stories. You can also offer "mini-lessons" on aspects of writing. Observe students' writing carefully to choose aspects of writing that suit your students' needs and interests. For example, in a mini-lesson students could share their knowledge about how to use phonics cues to encode words (invented spelling). Or, children could examine the opening sentences in several favorite storybooks and discuss different ways to begin a story (strong opening sentences).

Not all pieces of writing need to be revised. The only writing that will be revised will be that for which the student has a purpose or is particularly fond. It is important for you to work with your students to select those pieces of writing they will revise. Students are more likely to make corrections and rewrite work if they have participated in the selection of what will be revised, and if they are excited about what they are writing.

Step 5 Editing

Now students make the writing conform with the expectations of the reader; that is, they clean up the mechanics. Working with peers as well as the teacher, students examine their writing for spelling and usage errors.

You may wish to create a list with your students of things they should check when they are editing their work. You might start with one item and then add an additional item each week. For example, during the first week of school you may wish to make students responsible for the correct use of capital letters, during the second week the correct use of periods, etc. This list should be posted in a prominent place in the classroom and can serve as your style book.

Step 6 Publishing

Finally, those pieces that the writer has wanted to share more widely are presented or published. Class books and posters are effective ways to help young children publish frequently and to celebrate their authorship. Children's individual work should also be published and displayed. A variety of ways to publish students' work includes:

- displaying it on the wall
- binding it in Big Books, Little Books, and Accordion Books
- mailing letters
- recording students reading their own work on audio or video tape
- compiling it in class anthologies

Remember . . .

To ensure success:

- Celebrate every child's attempts to write.

- Provide ample materials so that students are able to create their own writing. Set up a writing center with a variety of writing materials, including pens, pencils, and paper. Students should be free to write at any time; they should not have to wait for a special time or an assignment to write.

- Brainstorming writing topics and preparing idea clusters is an excellent prewriting activity.

- Revision is not an exercise to be done for the purposes of the teacher, but rather for the writer.

- Similarly, editing is not an exercise to be done for the teacher, but rather when the writing is going to go on to a further audience, to be "published."

- Above all, show genuine interest in what students have to say.

Content-Area Instruction

Incorporating content-area instruction in language lessons helps ESL students become successful in their other classes. Emphasis throughout the lessons should be on acquiring the language necessary to participate in activities and on problem solving and discovery in the areas of science, math, social studies, and music and art.

Science

An activity-oriented program in which students are involved in experiments is the best way to accomplish the development of the cognitive abilities needed to understand scientific processes and learn the content. In these experiments students can collect data, learn to generalize from the data, and form and test hypotheses. Because of the concrete nature of the activity and their personal involvement, students are eager and enthusiastic—much more than they would be if they watched an experiment or read about it. This is particularly appropriate to the second-language learner, since strong visual and hands-on experiences make low-level linguistic demands. (Cantoni-Harvey, 1987)

Students who have had schooling in another culture in which memorization of facts and role learning were the manner of teaching may initially be reluctant to actively participate. However, as they watch other students take part, they will gradually become more comfortable with hands-on activities.

A teacher can find a number of ways to get around the language barrier with ESL students. For example, help students understand a lesson about magnets by presenting it in simple language supported by visual cues. If students are unable to answer questions verbally, they can show their understanding of which objects a magnet will or will not attract by holding up or pointing to pictures of real objects. When they are able to respond orally, they may begin to answer questions such as "Will a magnet pull a [nail, eraser, pencil, dime]?" As fluency develops, they can briefly explain the difference between the objects a magnet will and will not attract. As literacy develops, they can record their findings in writing. Remember these key points:

- Help pupils write and illustrate a dictionary of terms, the names of living things, words for weather, parts of the body, and so on.

- Use real materials, objects, and apparatus to demonstrate concepts or principles.

- Teach the special language of the scientist, particularly the verbs: *discover, observe, note, investigate, research, test, measure, find, prove, change,* etc.

- Give practice in reading cause and effect relationships and the *if . . . then* language that signals them.

- Provide students practice in the process of reading and checking information with graphs, charts and diagrams that accompany print.

- Ask students to keep written records of scientific events, such as a chronicle of the space flights or a weekly weather log.

- Contrast interrogative sentences, negative, and affirmative statements drawn from a science lesson.

- Develop a list of cognates drawn from the universal vocabulary of science. Help students find words in English that look like, or are similar to, words in their first language.

Mathematics

Students must learn how to solve problems but they must also learn specialized mathematical vocabulary. The ESL teacher should know what is being taught in the regular math class and find ways to introduce simplified vocabulary and concepts that the student will later need to be able to deal with. In many cases an ESL student may understand the concept but be unable to deal with the vocabulary of word problems. For example, the question "What was left?" could confound many students who think of *left* as only the antonym of *right*. Understanding the difference between divided by and divided into is crucial to a correct answer.

For students in elementary classes hands-on activities are most appropriate. Cantoni-Harvey (1987) observes:

> By playing with blocks of different color, shape, size, and thickness, the children construct mental representations of abstract attributes such as green and round. . . . As they arrange objects into groups by trial and error they will establish some criteria for categorizing them, and become able to describe and compare their distinctive features. Finally, they can learn to translate their verbal statements into symbols.

It is essential for the teacher to make sure the input is comprehensible throughout the activity, since language acquisition only takes place when the level of comprehension is high. Remember these key points:

- Have students prepare file cards of number words with the symbol on one side and the number word on the other.

- Have students prepare file cards for operations (add/+, subtract/−, etc.).
- Teach measurements by having students use actual instruments and devices whenever possible.
- Use coins and currency to teach monetary units.
- Use realistic situations to demonstrate concepts of increase/decrease, raise/lower, etc.
- Teach comparison words necessary to understanding and interpreting quantitative relationships: *more, less, most, least, larger, greater than, equal to,* etc.
- Rewrite word problems in simple English. Use short sentences, pictures, known symbols, and other illustrations that give meaning.
- Teach prefixes peculiar to the language of mathematics: *bi-, deci-, centi-, kilo-,* etc.
- Watch for the kinds of errors students make. Differentiate between the errors that result from lack of English comprehension and those that result from operational, computational, or conceptual inadequacies. Have tutors assist accordingly.

Social Studies

As a basis for comparing cultures, members of an ESL class can discuss their own lives and cultures, their holidays, food, and customs. These can be compared with the cultures of the United States, which they are experiencing, but not necessarily understanding. The teacher can often help the children find common surface threads—the way clothing varies according to use and climate, and so on.

In the elementary grades, students need many firsthand experiences. They can visit stores and other public places, and come back and draw, discuss, and write about what they saw and did. The teacher can take material from the regular social studies curriculum and books and present simplified versions to the ESL students. In this way students can gradually acquire vocabulary and knowledge that is appropriate to their grade level, even though it is in a less complete form. Remember these key points:

- Use students as cultural "informants;" compare, contrast, and celebrate the different cultures they represent.
- Help students build individual card files of needed terms.
- Teach the ways to construct a table from a set of data.

- Prepare a glossary of proper names and places.
- Keep a notebook of information about the history or geography of the country of the student.
- Be alert to concepts and values that may be unclear in written materials because of cultural differences.
- Prepare difficult passages of the textbooks on tape for listening and for following along.
- Provide tutorial assistance in the primary language to develop abstract concepts that are difficult to convey in English alone.

Music and Art

The most important feature of the arts curriculum to ESL teaching is the nonlinguistic transfer of emotional values and excitement. The pure pleasure shared by students who cannot yet voice that excitement or emotion is wonderful for ESL students.

Both music and art should be completely integrated into the ESL classroom at the elementary level. When students join in a song they are actively learning in many language areas. They are developing vocabulary, some of which may be new; they are learning stress and intonation patterns and rising and falling "tunes." Above all, students should enjoy music and art activities and should never be made to think of them as exercises. Remember these key points:

- Music and art should be included whenever appropriate to a lesson.
- Fingerplays, chants, and songs that encourage movement, and predictable, repetitious songs that children can readily join in on all serve different purposes and joyful learning.
- Art in the form of charts and graphs is especially appropriate to math and science lessons.
- Encourage students who are not yet able to write in English to draw pictures to express themselves.
- Encourage students to share songs from their cultures with classmates.

Remember . . .

To ensure success:

- Focus the lesson by designing a lesson plan that will present a general view of the topic and will focus on a few main ideas.

- Prepare accompanying visuals, pictures, charts, and graphs to provide supporting or alternative presentations of the information to be covered.

- For older students, prepare study sheets of key terms, and limit the list to those terms with a high probability of repetition in discussion and text.

- Incorporate the use of realia as much as possible.

- Use a tape recorder for individualized lessons that are geared to the student's language ability.

- Model all tasks to ensure comprehension.

- Encourage cooperative learning.

- Test broad concepts and, if possible, information relevant to the student's life and experience.

- Devise methods of having students demonstrate what they know.

The Role of Literature

Background

Experiences with fine literature help students develop an awareness and appreciation of the beauty of the English language. Stories, poems, and other forms of literature bring a wide range of language and cultural benefits to the ESL classroom.

Stories exist in all cultures, and children have heard them in their first language; it is a comfortable, familiar form. Howard Sage (1987) says, "Because they are already familiar with the concept of the story line, they feel more comfortable with stories and freer to react spontaneously to them, both positively and negatively." He suggests that students will want to write similar stories, changing the order of the events and, perhaps, changing the outcome of the story.

Probably the most important element in storytelling is the ability of the story to entertain, to enthrall the reader. In order to entertain, stories make use of colorful language and language devices such as metaphor, repetition, surprise endings, plot twists—all designed to heighten the reader's interest. Children who enjoy and comprehend stories will become readers.

Children's stories are designed to be clearly understood, and that clarity is reinforced by the illustrations. There is research that shows that stories convey the most easily understood messages, thus becoming excellent teaching devices. ". . . they meet current views that a comprehensible message reinforces learning languages by keeping students' anxiety levels down and self-esteem high." (Sage, 1987)

While students are enjoying stories, poems, rhymes, and other literature, they are learning about everyday life in the new culture. A story can provide a setting in which the ESL student can see how the new culture works. At the same time, learning rhymes, fairy stories, and folk tales of the new culture helps the second language learner fill in the gaps of the language references that other children already know.

Poetry is one natural route to expressing feelings. These feelings are in the words of the poem but are also in the response of the reader or listener. Emotions are touched by the ideas of the poem, and also by the figurative language and the sounds of alliteration and onomatopoeia. Students who are shy about oral work will often join in to read poems aloud. Traditional poetic forms, as do songs, clearly mark stress patterns and sentence intonation, and more often than not, rhyme.

It is important for the ESL learner to know that there are many ways to use language. So often students deal with nonfiction that uses language solely to impart information. Literature uses language for many other purposes—to amuse, to convince, to dream. Only through reading can students learn how to use the many resources of the language. Betty Smallwood (1991) points out that in stories children discover the different registers of language that they can then use themselves when they write. Remember these key points:

- Use predictable, repetitious stories — especially with beginners.
- Read aloud to your students as often as possible. Encourage parents to do the same — in their native language and in English.
- Provide a large variety of reading experiences for students with the various literary forms: poems, rhymes and jingles, stories, plays, etc.
- These pieces of literature serve as springboards for students' own creative writing.
- Encourage students to use various literary forms in their own writing.
- Have students read traditional stories from their cultures.
- If possible, provide and allow students to read literature in their first language.
- Encourage students to share with their classmates stories they have read or been told in their first language.
- Have students listen to and compare the same folk or fairy tale as told in versions from several different cultures.

Remember . . .

To ensure success:

- Provide a comfortable reading corner that invites students to read for their own enjoyment.
- As you share literature, use the model of the bedtime story—a warm, positive time with children.
- Encourage participation, but allow children to choose their own level of involvement.
- Encourage students to create new verses to predictable poems and songs.
- "Publish" childrens' work.

PART 2 Approaches and Techniques: Video Segments and Activities

Total Physical Response

Background

Total Physical Response (TPR) uses many of the same strategies that students use in acquiring their first language to enable them to acquire a second language. The focus on natural acquisition strategies makes the task of language learning enjoyable by combining visual, auditory, and kinesthetic learning modalities. You will enjoy using TPR because you can evaluate students' language comprehension as they participate actively and have fun.

Because the activities reinforce the linguistic concept, TPR makes language meaningful for students. Students receive meaningful input as the speaker demonstrates verbal commands for them.

Total Physical Response presents the beginning student with commands for physical actions, often combined with music, mime, or drama. At this point, the students may not be able to produce the language of the commands, but they can understand and follow them. James Asher based TPR on observations of first language acquisition, noting that for the first year or two of their lives children produce little or no language, but clearly respond to imperatives given by the adults around them.

> . . . listening skill is far in advance of speaking. For instance, it is common to observe young children who are not yet able to produce more than one-word utterances, yet they demonstrate perfect understanding when an adult says, "Pick up your red truck and bring it to me!". . . . We infer from these observations that it is no accident that listening precedes speaking. . . . Utterances, usually commands from adults, are used to manipulate the orientation, location, and locomotion of the child's entire body. This phenomenon can be observed in a

massive number of commands such as: "Come here! Stand still! " (Asher, 1979)

Asher has connected his theories with those of Stephen Krashen's natural language approach. Asher suggests that there is no anxiety for the child because there is no pressure to produce language at the beginning. The message is always clearly presented, using whatever body language or other cues necessary to communicate.

> The Total Physical Response approach does not limit the teacher to the simple physical commands, such as walking, stopping, jumping, often used with beginning students. More complex commands can be used with more advanced students. For example: ". . . find the picture of the woman with green eyes, long black hair and wearing a sun hat that has red stripes. When you find the picture, show it to the class. . . ." (Asher, Kusudo, and de la Torre, 1983)

A natural progression is to begin with TPR in which the teacher says and demonstrates the commands. When students are able to follow the commands easily, they can repeat the commands to fellow students. As a further development, students can make up commands from the language they have acquired.

The Basics—Implementing TPR

1. Teacher says and models the meaning of new vocabulary words or phrases. (For example: Touch your toes. Touch your nose.) Students respond by doing the action.

2. Teacher commands and models with a large group, a small group, and then with an individual volunteer.

3. Teacher commands without modeling and has a large group, a small group, and a volunteer respond by doing the action.

4. Teacher recombines old and new commands with and without modeling, and large and small groups and a volunteer respond by doing the action. (Touch your nose. Touch you toes.)

If students display any confusion during steps 3 and 4, immediately return to modeling the actions for them.

> *Remember...*
>
> To ensure success:
>
> 1 Allow a comfortably long receptive period. The length of this period will vary, student to student.
>
> 2. Change the order of commands to increase interest.
>
> 3. Change the groups commanded and always select them in an unanticipated order (small group, large group, pairs, individual, etc.). Students' listening and interest is much keener when they cannot anticipate whether they are next to perform.
>
> 4. Check for understanding to ensure that students are not just imitating you. (Step 4 allows you to do this.)
>
> 5. After sufficient practice, allow students to issue the commands.

Video Segment: TPR in Action

Pre-view Notes

As you watch this video segment, notice:

- how students exhibit various levels of language proficiency
- how the teacher chooses to introduce the activity
- how the teacher models the language and checks understanding
- how students have prepared for their performance and show understanding of the commands
- how the teacher reinforces polite social skills
- how the teacher delegates and encourages students to problem-solve on their own but takes control when necessary

Post-View Discussion

Work individually or in small groups to explore answers to these questions.

1. How were visual, auditory, and kinesthetic learning strategies present?

   visual _____

   auditory _____

   kinesthetic _____

2. TPR was used to practice and establish an essential language skill. What is the primary language skill/objective of the lesson?

   _____

   _____

3. How could the activity be extended or adapted?

   _____

   _____

   _____

   _____

Application Activities

Work in small groups. Elect a leader and spokesperson(s) to present your teaching plan. Make a teaching plan that uses TPR for one of the following activities.

- How to make a peanut butter and jelly sandwich
- Establishing vocabulary for classroom furniture and areas
- How to use a cassette player
- *Addison-Wesley ESL*, Level D, "The Workers' Song," pages 24–25

The Natural Approach

Background

The natural approach is a communicative-based method that recognizes that the acquisition of a second language is very much like the acquisition of one's primary language. The natural approach facilitates the acquisition of a second language in a natural way. Steve Krashen distinguishes between language acquisition and learning.

> . . . acquisition is a subconscious process that is identical to the process in first language acquisition in all important ways. While acquisition is taking place, the acquirer is not always A-Ware of it, and he or she is not usually A-Ware of its results. Learning is conscious knowledge, or 'knowing about' language. (Krashen, 1985)

Steve Krashen and Tracy Terrell have further described the major characteristics of the natural approach.

Comprehensible Input: Students aquire language when it is understandable or comprehensible. Students must understand the intent of the message, not necessarily every word that is spoken. Language is made comprehensible to students when teachers use visuals, media, body language and gestures—whatever will convey meaning to students.

Low Affective Filter: Students acquire language when they are engaged in an activity and their anxiety level is lowered. The classroom must be a safe, comfortable, supportive environment in which students feel free to take risks in using a second language.

Meaningful Communication: Students acquire language when they use it for real purposes. The language they use must be relevant, meaningful, and authentic. The focus is always function (getting things done with language) over form (grammatical structures).

Terrell stresses the importance of authentic communicative activities in the language classroom.

> Such activities allow the development of communicative abilities through natural acquisition processes in addition to fostering the kind of knowledge that results from conscious cognitive learning exercises. . . .
>
> Research indicates that acquisition takes place under certain conditions. In a communicative situation: (1) the focus of the interchange is on the message; (1) the acquirer must understand the message, and (3) the acquirer must be in a low-anxiety situation. (Terrell, 1983)

The Basics—Implementing the Natural Approach

Speech Emerges in Stages: Language acquisition and production proceeds through a series of natural stages.

1. **Preproduction** (a listening stage): The student can comprehend second language commands, but cannot yet speak the language.

   - Allow time for students to develop their receptive comprehension skills before you expect them to speak. Provide opportunities for them to listen to language that is made clear to them by means of pictures, objects, and gestures. Ask "yes/no" and alternative questions that can be answered with body language. Use TPR; respect the "silent" period many students need before risking speech.

2. **Early production:** Students comprehend more complicated language and can now make simple responses, such as yes/no and names.

   - Select activities that give students pleasure in using language, that are meaningful, and that allow students to respond with short answers.

   - Paraphrase one-word answers; put them into full sentences; let students listen to languge they cannot yet produce.

3. **Speech emergence:** Comprehension has increased and students can now speak in phrases and sentences.

   - Give students opportunities to speak in phrases and sentences. Encourage them to speak and interact using natural language in which the focus is on the message that is being communicated.

   - Provide activities that allow students to practice the language by role-playing specific messages.

   - Continue to model, model, model. Read aloud daily.

4. **Intermediate fluency:** Students combine phrases and sentences into expression that is both oral and written.

   - Provide activities that encourage students to respond with increasingly complex sentences, such as paraphrasing a story they have read or heard.

   - Use process-writing activities to stimulate creative imaginations and to introduce grammar and mechanics as students edit their work.

To summarize, the most effective language classroom is one in which students understand what is being communicated, the communications are always meaningful, and the atmosphere is supportive, relaxed and anxiety-free.

> *Remember...*
>
> To ensure success:
>
> - Create an environment in which students speaking experiences are positive and nonthreatening—the more they enjoy speaking, the more they will speak. Give positive feedback to every effort.
> - Assist students in comprehension by providing a wealth of clues—visual, auditory and kinesthetic. Do what you must to make the message understandable.
> - Maintain an anxiety-free class environment. Reward students for all attempts at communicating. Model correct forms rather than overtly correcting students.
> - Make communication the focus of all language activities. Avoid drills that do not use authentic language.
> - Work from the simple to the complex; always begin with easy questions (yes/no; alternative), and build to more difficult (information; inferential).

Video Segment: The Natural Approach in Action

Pre-view Notes

As you watch this video segment, notice:
- the various learning and teaching strategies used in the lesson; does the teacher use TPR?
- the different levels of student response
- the way the teacher moves from the simple to the complex

Post-view Discussion

Work in small groups to explore answers to these questions.

1. What stages of acquisition have students reached? Cite specific examples.

_____

_____

_____

2. How did the teacher provide comprehensible input?

3. How would you describe the classroom atmosphere?

4. How did the teacher and class give positive feedback and build self-confidence?

5. What assessment opportunities did you see?

6. How did the teacher work from the simple to the complex?

7. Did students' own poems rhyme? Does it matter?

8. What special event happens every week at this school? How might being chosen for it affect an ESL student?

_____

_____

_____

Application Activities

Work in small groups. Elect a leader and spokesperson(s) to present your teaching plan. Make a teaching plan that uses the Natural Approach for one of the following activities.

- Shared reading of a Big Book.
- Shared reading of a comic strip.
- Shared reading of another poem.
- *Addison-Wesley ESL* Level A, "The Peanut Butter and Jelly Song," page 44

The Language Experience Approach

NOTE: LEA has much in common with the two approaches that follow. Notice how these approaches overlap in both philosophy and classroom procedures.

Background

The Language Experience approach uses the student's own words as the material for beginning reading and then for writing. These famous lines apply to second-language learners as well as first-language learners:

> What I can think about I can talk about.
> What I can say I can write.
> What I can write I can read.
> I can read what I write and what other people write for me to read.
> Roach Van Allen (1961)

Cantoni-Harvey (1987) says, "No mass-produced texts can ever reflect an individual's experiences, interests, and language as accurately as the stories he creates." In the Language Experience approach students share an experience and discuss it. Then they dictate a story based on that experience. Because the material comes from their own knowledge, it is comprehensible and interesting to the student. This approach is especially appropriate for second language learners because the language generated is based on actual shared experiences and does not assume that students come from a single cultural or linguistic background.

R. V. Allen lists the following features, among others, of the Language Experience approach:

- There is no need to separate children into ability groups for direct instruction in reading skills.

- The concept load in reading material is eliminated when students use their own writing to learn to recognize words. They know what they are reading because they dictated or wrote it.

- Students with backgrounds of experience that are extremely divergent from the typical story content of books are not placed at a disadvantage. From the beginning they deal with ideas that are familiar and language that is theirs.

- This approach takes advantage of the wide variety of reading materials already available (basal texts, trade books, supplementary texts, newspapers, magazines). It does not require the purchase of extensive quantities of new story material.

- Language experience emphasizes use of multisensory materials, such as filmstrips, recordings, and tapes.
- Students express themselves in multiple media: talking, writing, rhythms, art forms, and dramatization. Their personal, individual ideas are valued in any form of self-expression they select for communication.
- Reading is treated as a process of reconstructing oral language that has been written.

The Basics—Implementing the Language Experience Approach

1. Share and discuss an experience. This can be a field trip, a science experiment, a cooking project, a classroom visitor, a game, a story. A common experience provides much to talk about. Allow plenty of time for discussion. Discussion will bring out key vocabulary and a cluster of ideas students can use as they dictate their language experience story.

2. After the discussion, encourage the class to dictate a story. Individual students can contribute words, phrases, and/or sentences. Write legibly on an overhead projector, on chart paper, or on a chalkboard. If you wish, ask questions to help structure the story, for example: *Where did you go? What did you see?*

    Write the children's words exactly as they are spoken. Sometimes language experience stories are written as running narratives. Sometimes they are presented as a series of quotes:
    Lia said, "I liked the zebra best."
    Tommy said, "I liked the baby giraffe."

3. Read the story together and consider revisions. Model the revision process by pointing out elements of the story that you recall like: lots of details, descriptive word choice, a unifying closing sentence, etc. Encourage children to talk about things they like about the story, too. Ask children if there is anything they would like to change in their story to make it even better. Most young children will like their story exactly the way it is, and that's fine. At times you may want to suggest a focus for revision, for example, reordering sentences into chronological sequence. If you have written the story on chart paper, you can cut the sentences apart for children to physically reorder.

4. Read and reread the story. Point to the words as you read the story aloud with the class. Then, let volunteers point to the words as the class reads together. Some students may want to point to

and read the words they contributed themselves. Groups of students or individuals may want to read selected parts of the story to the class.

Using Language Experience Stories to Explore Aspects of Print

Language experience charts and books provide a meaningful context for exploring aspects of print and developing early reading skills. If you laminate your language experience chart, children can use markers to circle words and letters, then wipe the chart clean with a damp paper towel. Choose activities that interest and are appropriate for individuals or groups of students. Here are some sample activities:

- Have children look for certain recurring words, words beginning with a given letter, etc.
- Noting capital letters and final punctuation marks, have children count the number of sentences.
- Make sentence strips. Have students order the sentence strips to match the language experience chart.
- Make word cards. Have students order the word cards to match the sentence on a page of a language experience Big Book.

Remember . . .

To ensure success:

- Almost anything can be the basis for a Language Experience story, as long as the language and vocabulary are fully developed.
- Always have chart paper, sentence strips, and pencils ready at hand. You may wish to set up a Language Experience center that is stocked with a tape recorder, tapes, drawing paper, and crayons.
- Train volunteers to record Language Experience stories from children—in English or in the student's first language.

Video Segment: The Language Experience Approach in Action

Pre-view Notes

As you watch this video segment, notice:

- how the teacher uses different ideas and visuals to build oral language skills.
- how the oral discussion prepares the children for the story-telling.
- how the teacher writes the children's words exactly as they are spoken.
- how students at different stages of language acquisition are able to participate.

Post-view Discussion

Work in small groups to explore answers to these questions.

1. What were the common denominators—the familiar, shared experiences—the teacher used to motivate and prepare children for the storytelling and writing activities?

   _____
   _____
   _____

2. What visual "props" carried the story telling? Why were they important?

   _____

3. How did the teacher elicit language and keep the children's storytelling moving?

   _____
   _____
   _____

4. How could the activity be expanded?

_____

_____

_____

Application Activities

Work in groups of four. Make a teaching plan that uses the Language Experience Approach for one of the following activities.

- A shared reading of a Big Book
- Discussion of a common holiday (Halloween, Thanksgiving)
- A "pollution hunt" around the school grounds
- *Addison-Wesley ESL*, Level D, page 54

Integrated Language Teaching

Background

Integrated Language Teaching focuses on using language rather than learning language. Language is acquired in whole-meaning chunks; it is not broken down into small unrelated segments. Language experience, both oral and written, should be interwoven with the instruction in all curriculum areas throughout the day.

Enright and McCloskey (1988) give seven theoretical assumptions of the Integrated Language Teaching model.

1. Language is to be viewed as a whole, and not taught in small discrete "skills."

2. Language and literacy are developed through use of language as a tool rather than through study of language as a subject (e.g., language arts).

3. Students need a great deal of input of language they can understand, and that is interesting and useful.

4. All the language processes work together to help acquisition of each. So students need to use listening, speaking, reading, and writing as part of a whole, rather than as separate skills.

5. Students bring experiences in language and culture to their task of learning a second language.

6. Language is used in many different ways, depending on the purpose and the user and receiver. Students need to have experience with this wide variety.

7. An accepting and relaxed atmosphere is necessary for good language acquisition.

Following this theoretical model, the classroom becomes a place where active language learning is going on at all times, not just when it is being deliberately taught as a "lesson." The teacher can make use of the students' previous experiences as building blocks in learning the new language.

The Basics—Implementing Integrated Language Teaching

1. Choose a theme that incorporates both the students' and the teacher's interests.

2. Brainstorm to form a web diagram that ties together ideas from many sources into your teaching theme. Developing a web of ideas that stem from a central word or theme highlights the connection among different disciplines and skills. As opposed to a list, in which each idea leads to the next, a web allows a number of ideas to appear at the same time, even if they are not directly related.

   The final web will likely contain more subtopics and curriculum areas for exploring than you can use for your lesson, but the possibilities you create provide opportunities for subsequent activities. For example, the following model web for Grandparents sets the stage for the storytelling activity "Naughty Marisia," seen in the LEA video segment.

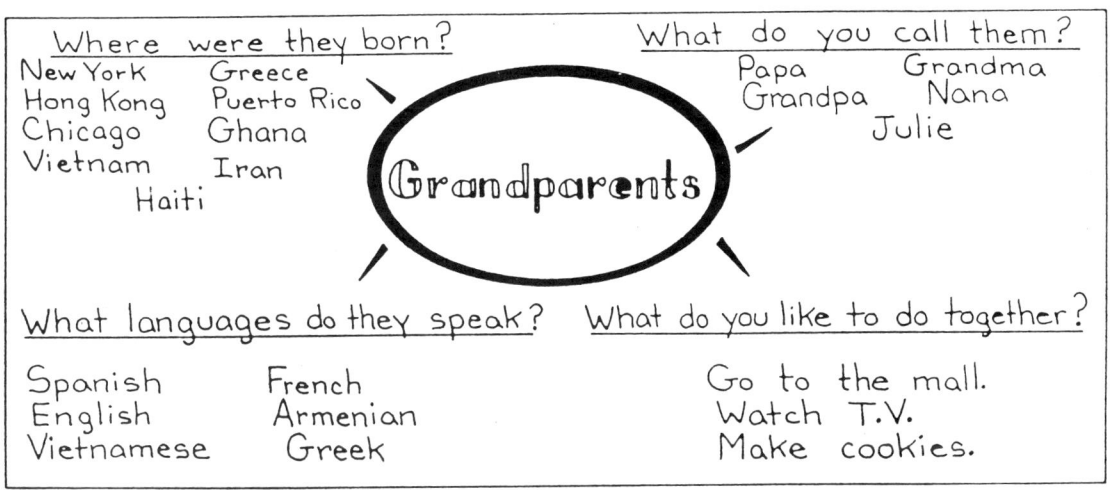

from TLLC by McCloskey, Hooper, Linse

3. Semantic mapping is a higher level of brainstorming in which students and teachers work together to make connections between the ideas they have grouped together and the topic word. After the maps have been made, students can write about the contrasts and comparisons they find in the map. Semantic maps encourage students to make the bridge from the abstract to the concrete. (Anderson-Curtain and Pesola, 1988)

4. Use all the skills of language—listening, speaking, reading, and writing—as a total process.

5. Celebrate and incorporate students' cultural heritage.

6. Provide a welcoming atmosphere that encourages students to experiment and work with language. Provide ready access to fine literature. Create a reading area that invites children to read their favorite books. Encourage students to bring to the classroom and talk about objects that are representative of their life outside the classroom.

> *Remember . . .*
>
> To ensure success:
>
> - Present language as a tool that helps students think, problem solve, and successfully attack other learning tasks.
> - Teach language as a total process of listening, speaking, reading, writing . . . and critical thinking.
> - Celebrate and incorporate students' cultural heritage into the learning activities.
> - Provide an inviting classroom atmosphere that is conducive to language acquisition.

Video Segment: Integrated Language Teaching in Action

Pre-view Notes

As you watch this video segment, notice:

- how listening, speaking, reading, and writing are used as a total process
- how brainstorming a web/semantic mapping is used as a prewriting activity
- how students show understanding of figurative language

Post-view Discussion

Work in small groups to explore answers to these questions.

1. Was this lesson based on a concrete experience of student involvement? Explain.

   _____
   _____
   _____

2. How did the teacher motivate interest in the lesson?

   _____
   _____
   _____

3. What techniques and strategies already discussed did you see? Explain.

   _____
   _____
   _____
   _____

4. Give examples of how the students proved understanding of similes and metaphors.

   a metaphor they created _____

   a simile they created _____

5. How could the activity be extended or adapted?

   _____
   _____
   _____

6. Choose any emotion. Create your own simile or metaphor.

   _____
   _____
   _____

Work in groups of four. Make a teaching plan that uses Integrated Language Teaching for one of the following activities.

Application Activities

- Writing a collaborative essay about a beautiful (or stormy) day
- Dinosaurs
- Planning (and reporting back about) a field trip to a museum
- *Addison-Wesley ESL*, Level D, "Ears Hear," page 119

Whole Language

Background

Like Integrated Language Teaching, Whole Language unites the strands of language learning. Whole Language instruction emphasizes meaningful and enjoyable communication through natural acquisition.

Activities in this approach come in all modes, from reading to discussing to writing down the discussion ideas.

> . . . the children's writing and authorship are integrated with a reading program of children's literature. Whole, meaningful texts are the instructional materials, not isolated words, sound, or vocabulary-controlled "stories." In a Whole Language classroom, oral and written language must be functional, fulfilling a particular purpose for the language use. (Edelsky, Draper, and Smith, 1983)

The use of Big Books and shared book experiences is one of the most successful strands of the Whole Language approach. This extends the practice of reading aloud to reading aloud from Big Books. These books use predictable, repetitive phrases to catch the student's ear and wonderful, lively art to catch the student's eye. Holdaway (1973) is one of the chief proponents of Big Books:

> Gathered around a book as a natural, sharing community, children learn more from actual participation than from direct instruction; they learn from the teacher's model, from their own sensible involvement, and from each other, without any sense of competition or pressure.

Big Books are used as the stimulus for a world of language and print. Beverly Wilkins (1984) writes of the way one such program works.

> During story repetitions, the teacher pauses to emphasize print conventions or to mask over a word or phrase, asking the children to predict what comes next. She varies the instruction according to the skills already possessed by the children. . . .
> Later the children take small versions of the large book and go over them alone or in small groups. Always they wish to write books themselves, beginning with a simple imitation of the story that the teacher presents and ending up desiring to create a story of their own. . . .

The Whole Language approach is based on function before form and moves from whole to part. It recognizes that language is the same in and out of school and that language development is a holistic personal-social achievement.

The Basics—Implementing Whole Language

1. Provide shared reading experiences that allow students to listen to a story and participate by joining in with story refrains.

2. Use Big Books, or other enlarged print materials, that help students see and understand the correspondence between spoken and written words.

3. Select stories that make new vocabulary easily understood and acquired through the meaningful context of a predictable story and the use of repeated language patterns.

4. Encourage students to talk about the story or to retell the story using picture cues.

5. Extend understanding through related reading, oral, and written activities that further explore the concepts or theme of the story.

How to Make Your Own Big Books and Poem Charts

Inspiration and Sources for Big Books

1. Children can use the language patterns and story structure of simple, predictable books and poems to create their own derivative stories and poems. Most young children enjoy this type of "innovation" enormously and get great satisfaction out of creating their own Big Books or Poem Posters.

2. Children can retell stories in their own words and illustrate each scene. Language experience stories can be divided into pages and illustrated to make a class Big Book.

3. Big Books can be created from songs and poems. Write the words in enlarged type, dividing the poem or song at logical breaking points. Let children illustrate. Standard sized books can also be made into Big Books for classroom use. Choose books with simple, predictable text and rewrite the text in enlarged type. If the book illustrations are large enough, you can buy two paperback copies of the book and use the original art to illustrate each page.

Materials for Making Big Books

1. The print on Big Books and Poem Posters should be large and clear to read. You can use dark-colored markers to print the words, or use a large font program on a computer, such as

Printshop by Broderbund or MagicSlate by Sunburst. If possible, reproduce the sentences line-for-line as they appear in logical, consistent places.

2. Large sheets of tagboard, bristol board, or other sturdy paper make durable Big Books that are easy for children to handle. Big Books and Poem Posters can also be made from butcher paper cut into page-sized sheets. For added stiffness, tape two sheets back to back with wide masking tape. After the pages are illustrated, they can be laminated for greater durability.

3. There are a number of ways to bind Big Books together. You can use wide masking or binding tape. Start with the last page (or back cover) of the book and tape each page to the one preceding it. When all pages are taped together, tape a final strip of strong colorful tape (Mystic tape) down the spine.

4. Holes can be punched and Big Books can be bound together with metal binder rings. These rings can be found in office supply stores. Shower curtain rings also work well.

5. If your school has a book binding machine. Big Books can also be neatly punched and bound with plastic comb bindings.

6. Big Books with chain or cummulative story lines often work well as accordion books. These can be displayed as wall murals or folded accordion-style and read as books.

Illustrating Big Books and Poem Posters

Offer a variety of different art media for illustrating Big Books and Poem Posters. If your Big Book is inspired by a story book, you may also want to use the illustrator's art style as inspiration. Art work can be mounted on the Big Book pages. Borders around the art work can give additional visual appeal. On Poem Posters, the children's art can form a wide border around the text. Experiment with different art materials and ways of presenting the children's art. For example,

- Torn and cut paper
- Markers, pastels, tempera paint, crayons, chalk
- Figures cut out and combined on a background collage; materials— yarn, buttons, wallpaper, foil, etc.
- photographs

Story Poem Posters and Big Books

Big Books made of tagboard or other sturdy paper can be stored on bookshelves or clipped to skirt hangers hanging on a rod. Poem Posters can have holes punched and metal rings attached. The rings can be attached to coat hangers hanging on a rod or a coat rack. Big Books with ring bindings can be hung by a single ring from a "cup hook," or attached to clothes hangers and stored on a coat rack.

Remember . . .

Learning a language is easy when:

- It's real and natural
- It's whole
- It's sensible
- It's interesting
- It's relevant
- It belongs to the learner
- It's part of a real event
- It has social utility
- It has purpose and meaning for the learner
- It's accessible to the learner
- The learner has the power to use it

Video Segment: The Whole Language Approach in Action

Pre-view Notes

As you watch this video segment, notice:

- How the lesson appeals to visual, auditory and kinesthetic modalities
- How the teacher moves from whole to part
- How the teacher works with conventions of print
- How the teacher gives positive feedback

Post-view discussion

1. How did the Big Book itself exemplify the Whole Language philosophy?

_____

_____

_____

2. How was the shared reading enhanced and extended?

_____

_____

_____

3. How was the song similar to the book?

_____

_____

_____

Application Activities

Work in groups of four. Make a teaching plan that uses the whole language approach for one of the following activities.
- A shared reading of Big Book, "The Three Little Pigs," or any Big Book
- Creating an original Big Book for older students
- *Addison-Wesley ESL*, Level C, "Dreams,"page 120,

Whole Language Assessment

A non-intrusive part of the learning day, whole language assessment focuses on the positive, documenting what each student knows and can do. Observe students at work and use multiple measures to get a rich picture of the capabilities of each student. By systematically gathering information and building portfolios of students' work, you will be able to evaluate growth over time, pinpoint areas of concern, and determine the most effective learning modes for individuals.

Checklists

Checklists can give clear answers to clear questions, are easy to use, and can be used with groups of students as well as individually. A checklist can help you determine answers to such questions as, "Is this student comprehending instructions?" "Is this student participating in Shared Reading?" "Is this student beginning to use punctuation marks?" "Which students are using which Learning Centers?"

Anecdotal Records

Anecdotal records are descriptions of students' actions written as they occur or soon afterwards. Try to simply describe what you see— save your analysis for later when you have collected additional information. Select events that are interesting and important for the student observed, but do not focus only on negative behavior. Whole Language assessment encourages us to focus on what our students can do and how they do it.

Some teachers find it convenient to use a clipboard and pages of adhesive labels. They write their observations on labels, date the labels and, later, transfer them to the appropriate student files. Be sure to keep your observation sheets and files secure and private.

To ensure that you observe all children systematically, check names off a class list as you record observations. At the end of each week, or every two weeks, glance at the names that have not been checked and focus on each of these students for a few minutes.

Periodically review the anecdotal records you have collected and reflect on them. These insights will help you plan activities and learning centers that reflect your students' interests, support their strengths, and meet their needs.

Audio and Video Recordings

Early in the school year and periodically throughout the year, make audio or video tapes of students talking, singing, "reading," putting on plays, etc. Remember to record the date at the beginning of each taping session. Use the tapes to review and assess students' language development and other progress through the year. You may wish to play segments for parents at conferences—they will be delighted to note their child's growth. Provide opportunities for students to listen to or watch the growth and change they see in themselves. (Note: Some children may not want to be tape recorded. You should, of course, respect their right to say no.)

If you do not have recording equipment or prefer not to use it, document students' language development by transcribing bits of conversations. Write down their speech, word for word. Note accompanying gestures and actions. Transcribe speech samples for students at least three times during the year.

Interviews and Conversations

Occasionally, conduct individual interviews with students. Do this in a non-intimidating manner. See if they can tell you their first and last names and their ages. Ask them other information questions. Tape record or transcribe the interviews. Engage the children in friendly conversations whenever possible. Give them an opportunity to tell you about their learning, their friends, their favorite classroom activity, their outside interests and lives. Include notes about these conversations in the students' files.

Student Portfolios

Select samples of students' art work, captions, and stories dictated by children, and original writings to include in their portfolios. Try to gather one work sample from each student each week. Carefully date items that you include. (You may want to have children date all their work with a stamp.) Both you and your students can choose the pieces to include in the portfolios. Set up an accessible filing system using file folders, expandable folders, or large envelopes kept in a file cabinet or milk crate. Ask students to help you keep the portfolios in chronological order by always placing their latest work in the front of the file.

Sometimes, you may choose to photocopy the child's work so he or she can take home the original. Review the students' portfolios periodically to be sure you have included samples of different types of written and dictated works.

Analyze the dictation samples to evaluate the students' use of vocabulary, language structure, and story structure and their ability to take the listener (or audience) into account. Review the students' written work—lists, picture captions, journal entries, notes to you, etc.—and note what children know and are learning about writing. Use the information to make educational decisions about how best to encourage and nurture your emergent writers. Throughout the year, encourage students to look through their portfolios, review favorite work from the past, and note how their writing skills have developed.

Sharing Portfolios and Cumulative Files with Parents and Concerned Colleagues

Student portfolios are very useful in teacher-parent conferences. As you show samples of their child's work collected over a period of time, parents will be able to see concrete examples of their child's progress. They will be able to discuss the work with you, ask specific questions, and perhaps give you some new insights on their child's work and learning style.

Cumulative files containing samples of work from students' portfolios, anecdotal observations, checklists, and selected audio or video recordings will provide other teachers involved with the students, including next year's teachers, with a rich history of each student's growth and achievements.

The Cognitive, Academic Language Learning Approach—CALLA

Background

The Cognitive, Academic Language Learning approach (CALLA)* helps students in the transition from an ESL program into the mainstream curriculum by teaching them the learning strategies needed to successfully handle content area material. These strategies assist intermediate and advanced students to understand and retain content area material while they are increasing their language skills. Even beginning language students can benefit from hands-on content lessons that don't demand sophisticated language abilities.

Chamot and O'Malley (1987) point out that content-based English language courses are actually more interesting to many students than classes that only teach English. The students enjoy being involved with "real" school work, and content material contains topics of high interest to students. At the same time they are developing essential academic language skills.

Each CALLA content area lesson consists of three parts:

1. Content: The content of a lesson is determined by the grade-level basal curriculum in science, math, social studies, etc.

2. Language: In order to deal with the content material the student must learn the language functions used in content classes, such as describing, classifying, explaining, etc. At this point, the student must also learn the grammatical structures and the specialized vocabulary of each content area.

3. Strategy: The learning strategy is the technique that will be emphasized and overtly taught during the lesson. These learning strategies are essential to mainstream success.

Examples of learning strategies:

Advance organization: Preview the main ideas of the material to be learned
Organizational planning: Planning the parts, sequence, and main ideas to be expressed
Selective attention: Attending to key words, phrases, or types of information
Self-monitoring: Checking one's comprehension or production while it is taking place

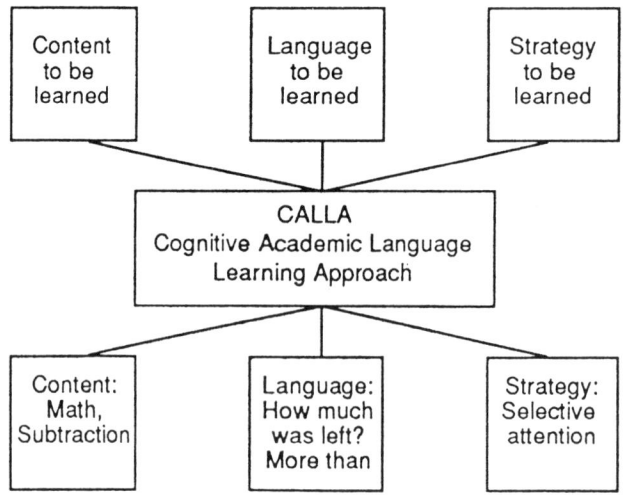

By integrating these types of language activities with grade-appropriate content, a curriculum based on the CALLA model can provide LEP students with the conceptual knowledge and language skills they will need to participate successfully in the mainstream classroom. (Chamot, 1985)

Self-evaluation: Judging how well one has accomplished a learning activity after it has been completed

Grouping: Classifying words or concepts according to their attributes

Note-taking: Writing down key words and concepts in verbal, graphic, or numerical form

Imagery: Using mental or actual images to understand and remember new information

Transfer: Using what is already known about language to assist comprehension or production

Elaboration: Relating new information to prior knowledge; relating different parts of new information; making personal associations

Inferencing: Using information in a text to guess meanings of new items or complete missing parts

Resourcing: Using reference materials such as dictionaries, encyclopedias, or textbooks

Cooperation: Working together with peers to solve a problem, pool information, check a learning task, or get feedback on oral or written performance

The Basics—Implementing CALLA

1. Develop a lesson plan that will present a general view of the topic and will focus on a few main ideas.

2. Prepare study sheets of key terms and concepts, and limit the list to those terms with a high probability of repetition in discussion and text.

3. Incorporate the use of realia as much as possible.

4. Use a language master or tape recorder for individualized lessons that are geared to the student's language ability.

5. Prepare accompanying visuals, pictures, charts, and graphs to provide supporting or alternative presentations of the information to be covered.

6. Test broad concepts and, if possible, information relevant to the student's life and experience.

Remember . . .

To ensure success:

- As lessons unfold, make sure students know which strategies they are using—and why.

- Encourage note-taking, outlining, and self-editing as students engage in oral and written expression.

- Encourage students to work cooperatively and independently on research and report projects.

- Take advantage of every opportunity to move from low-level questions that require recall of facts to high-level questions that require synthesis, analysis, and critical thinking.

Video Segment: CALLA in Action

Pre-view Notes

As you watch this video segment, notice:

- the irresistible pull of discovery in a hands-on activity
- the three parts of CALLA—content, language, and learning strategies in action
- how student interact and help each other

Post-view Discussion

1. Complete the diagram.

CALLA

Content	Language	Strategy
Science: solar motion, shadows Math: graphing	comparisons er/est; shorter/ taller than	Advance organization Elaboration Note-taking Cooperation

2. Which of the other approaches were also in action? Cite student and/or teacher behaviors.

_____
_____
_____

3. What skills did students need to successfully complete the activity?

_____
_____
_____

4. How did the teacher facilitate learning?

_____
_____
_____

Application Activities

Work in groups of four. Make a teaching plan that uses CALLA for one of the following activities.

- Classifying in the content area of science
- Reading a map
- Solving math and word problems
- *Addison-Wesley ESL*, Level D, "George Washington Carver," pages 60-63

The Functional-Notional Approach to Syllabus Design

Background

Language functions are uses of language such as requesting, asking for and giving information, commanding, agreeing, and so on. Language notions are the meanings that are expressed in that language. The Functional-Notional Approach was developed in reaction to purely grammatical teaching methods that teach structure for its own sake without regard to the communicative purpose it serves. It was developed by the Council of Europe (Van Ek, 1976) to help in the preparation of teaching materials for adult foreign language study.

> What people do by means of language can be described as verbally performing certain functions. . . . people assert, question, command, expostulate, persuade, apologize, etc. In performing such functions people express . . . certain notions. They will, for instance, apologize for being late, for being late for a party, etc. . . . Our task, then, . . . is to determine what language-functions the learners will have to be able to perform and what notions they will have to be able to handle (Van Ek, 1976)

The student discovers that there are a number of different ways to express the same functional purpose. The functional approach helps the student understand that these different ways of expressing meaning allow the speaker to show varying degrees of politeness, respect, and so on.

The Basics—
Implementing the Functional-Notional Approach

Role-playing, pairwork, and cooperative learning are excellent strategies to use with the Functional-Notional Approach. Task-based learning (Long, 1985) is a great example of the Functional-Notional Approach.

1. Identify target tasks (such as buying/selling bus, train, airline, and theater tickets).
2. Classify target tasks into task types (buying/selling tickets)
3. Derive pedagogical tasks. (For example: matching dialogue excerpts with locales, matching requests with ticket availability, identifying seat availability, unscrambling written dialogue, etc.)
4. Sequence the pedagogical tasks to form a task syllabus.
5. Evaluate achievement using task-based tests.

The Structural Approach to Syllabus Design

Background

The Structural Approach teaches the formal aspects of language, in particular, the rules for grammar. In the past, grammar was introduced at the beginning of language instruction; it was felt that students would develop bad habits if they didn't know the rules from the outset. With the development of the communicative methods, grammar came to be viewed as a set of explanations that could or should wait until oral language is established.

The distinction made by Krashen (1985) between acquisition and learning is also made by Asher (1983).

> The instructional model is to start with implicit learning (or acquisition) and gradually as the individual's understanding of the target language becomes more sophisticated make a transition to explicit learning.

Thus, when a student has acquired basic language and can communicate comfortably (acquisition), it is an appropriate time to introduce formal grammatical concepts (learning).

> Language structures should always be taught within context and in small increments in order for students to internalize their purpose. The structures of language should become a discovery process between teacher and student as they review or revise reading material. The study of language structures should never preclude the importance of meaning. Students need to see language in whole models first before they begin to examine each puzzle piece. (C. McElvain, 1990)

It is up to you to decide how much attention needs to be paid to the formal instruction of grammar. It is important that students learn how to communicate and feel comfortable with English. If students are presented with opportunities to hear correct English and participate in meaningful and enjoyable communication experiences, their English will improve. Students preparing for mainstream challenges DO need a firm grasp on grammar, however.

PART 3 — Culminating Video Segments and Activities

The video segments you viewed in the preceding section of this handbook were designed to illustrate unique features of a given instructional approach. In reality, effective teaching combines a variety of teaching strategies and approaches, and you've probably already noticed and discussed this. The next video segments focus on this integration of strategies and approaches.

Video Segment: Tip Top Adventures

Pre-view Notes

These high interest stories act as springboards for creative writing, but also serve another purpose.

As you watch the video, notice:

- how the teacher chooses to introduce and follow up the story
- the different ways in which the students read silently
- the different strategies and approaches in action

Post-view Discussion

1. Which approaches and strategies did you see? Give examples of teacher/student behaviors.

    ❏ TPR _____

    _____

    _____

    ❏ Integrated Language Teaching _____

    _____

    _____

    ❏ The Natural Approach _____

    _____

    _____

    _____

    ❏ Whole Language _____

    _____

    _____

    _____

❏ Language Experience _____

_____
_____
_____
_____

❏ CALLA _____

_____
_____
_____
_____

❏ Cooperative Learning _____

_____
_____
_____

❏ Process Writing _____

_____
_____
_____

❏ Content-area Instruction _____

_____
_____
_____

❏ Literature _____

_____
_____
_____

2. Which reading skills did the teacher reinforce in the follow-up discussion?

3. Tip Top stories were written to help students understand and use a certain grammar point. What is it? Why is it difficult for many students?

4. How could this lesson be extended or adapted?

Video Segment: Shape People/Kachina Dolls

Pre-view Notes

A kindergarten class and a third grade class work in different ways with colors and shapes.

As you watch the video, notice:

- the different multi-modal activities and levels of language abilities

- how the kindergarten teacher moves from the simple to the complex

- the various strategies and methods

- how language and concepts are introduced and re-introduced in a "spiral" fashion

Post-view Discussion

1. Give examples of teacher/student behaviors from the kindergarten class of:

   ❏ TPR _____

   _____

   _____

   ❏ Integrated Language Teaching _____

   _____

   _____

   ❏ The Natural Approach _____

   _____

   _____

   ❏ Whole Language _____

   _____

❏ Language Experience _____
_____

❏ CALLA _____
_____

2. Give examples of teacher/student behaviors from the third grade class of:

❏ TPR _____
_____

❏ Integrated Language Teaching _____
_____

❏ The Natural Approach _____
_____

❏ Whole Language _____
_____

❏ Language Experience _____
_____

❏ CALLA _____
_____

3. How did the kindergarten TPR segment move from the simple to the complex?

_____
_____
_____

4. Which modalities did you see?

_____
_____
_____

5. Which strategies did you see? If you didn't see one of the following, how could it be integrated?

   ❏ Cooperative Learning _____

   _____

   _____

   ❏ Process Writing _____

   _____

   _____

   ❏ Content-area Instruction _____

   _____

   _____

   ❏ Literature _____

   _____

   _____

6. Cite opportunities for assessment.

   Kindergarten: _____

   _____

   _____

   Third Grade _____

   _____

   _____

   _____

Video Segment: The Salt and Pepper Shake

Pre-view Notes

A kindergarten class and a second-grade class learn and respond to a song in different ways. Children shown are from mixed classrooms.

As you watch the video, notice:

- how the core activity can be used effectively from kindergarten through grade 2 . . . or beyond
- how students exhibit different stages of language acquisition
- how the second grade teacher uses a cloze procedure to model and check students' understanding
- the various strategies and approaches used in the two lessons

Post-view Discussion

1. Which approaches did you see? Give examples of teacher/student behaviors.

   ❏ TPR _____

   _____

   _____

   ❏ Integrated Language Teaching _____

   _____

   _____

   ❏ The Natural Approach _____

   _____

   ❏ Whole Language _____

   _____

   ❏ Language Experience _____

   _____

❏ CALLA _____
_____

2. What were the primary differences between the kindergarten and the second grade excerpts?

_____
_____
_____

3. Give examples of how the second grade teacher modeled the language and checked understanding.

_____
_____
_____

4. Which strategies did you see? Give examples of teacher/student behaviors. If you didn't see one of the following, how could it be integrated?

❏ Cooperative Learning _____
_____
_____

❏ Process Writing _____
_____
_____

❏ Content-area Instruction _____
_____
_____

❏ Literature _____
_____
_____

Video Segment: The Salt and Pepper Shake

5. How did the teacher facilitate during the group work?

_____
_____
_____

6. How could the lessons be extended or adapted?

_____
_____
_____

Bibliography

Bibliography

Allen, R.V., 1961. Report of the Reading Study Project, Monograph No.1. San Diego: Department of Education, San Diego Country.

Allen, R. V., and Allen, C. 1976. *Language experience activities.* Boston: Houghton Mifflin.

Anderson-Curtain, Helena and Pesola, Carol Ann, 1988. *Languages and children—Making the match.* Reading, MA: Addison-Wesley Publishing Company.

Asher, James J., 1979. *Learning another language through actions.* Los Gatos, CA: Sky Oaks Productions.

Asher, James J., 1983. Motivating children and adults to acquire a second language. In Oller and Richard-Amato.

Asher, James J., Kusudo, Jo Anne, and de la Torre, Rita., 1983.Learning a second language through commands: the second field test. In Oller and Richard-Amato.

Brigham Young University, 1990 *Culture grams.*

Brookes, Mona, 1986. *Drawing with children: A creative teaching and learning method that works for adults, too.* Los Angeles, CA: J.P. Tarcher.

California State Department of Education, 1987. *English-Language Arts Framework.* Sacramento, CA: California State Department of Education.

Calkins, L. M., 1983. *Lessons from a child.* Exeter, NH: Heinemann Educational Books.

Calkins, L. M., 1986. *The art of teaching writing.* Portsmouth, NH: Heinemann Educational Books.

Cantoni-Harvey, Gina, 1987. *Content-area language instruction.* Reading, MA: Addison-Wesley Publishing Company.

Chamot, A. U., 1985. English language development through a content-based approach. In *Issues in English language development.* Wheaton, MD: National Clearing House for Bilingual Education.

Chamot, A. U. and O'Malley, J. M., 1987. The cognitive academic language learning approach: A bridge to the mainstream. In *TESOL Quarterly,* 21, No. 2, June. Washington, DC: TESOL.

Chamot, A.U. and O'Malley, J.M., forthcoming. *The CALLA handbook.* Reading, MA: Addison-Wesley Publishing Company.

Cummins, J., 1983. "Language proficiency and academic achievement." In J. Oller (ed.) 1983 *Issues in Language Testing Research.* Rowley, MA: Newbury House.

Cook, Doris M., Ed., 1986. *A guide to curriculum planning in reading.* Madison, WI: Wisconsin Department of Public Instruction.

Edelsky, C., Draper, K., and Smith, K., 1983. Hookin 'em in at the start of school in a "whole language" classroom. *Anthropology and Education Quarterly,* 14(4).

Enright, D. Scott and McCloskey, Mary Lou, 1988. *Integrating English: Developing English language and literacy in the multilingual classroom.* Reading, MA: Addison-Wesley Publishing Company.

Goodman, K.S., Goodman, Y. M., and Hood, W. J., 1988. *The whole language evaluation book.* Portsmouth, NH: Heinemann.

Graves, D., 1983. *Writing: Teachers and children at work.* Exeter, NH: Heinemann Educational Books.

Johnson, D.W., Johnson, R.T., Holubec, E.J., and Roy, P., 1984. *Circles of learning: Cooperation in the classroom.* Alexandria, VA: Association for Supervision and Curriculum Development.

Holdaway, D., 1972. *Independence in reading: A handbook on individualized procedures.* Auckland, New Zealand: Ashton Education.

Holdaway, D. ,1979. *The foundations of literacy.* Sydney Australia: Ashton Scholastic (Available through Heinemann Educational Books, Portsmouth, NH).

Hyltenstam, K. and Pienemann, M., 1985. *Modelling and accessing second language proficiency.* Clevedon, Avon: Multilingual Matters.

Kagan, S., 1988. *Cooperative learning: resources for teachers.* Laguna Miguel, CA: Spencer Kagan, Ph.D.

Krashen, S. D., and Terrell, D., 1983. *The natural approach: language acquisition in the classroom.* Hayward, CA: Alemany Press.

Krashen, Stephen D., 1985. *Inquiries & insights.* Hayward, CA: Alemany Press.

Long, M. H., 1985. A role for instruction in second language acquisition task-based language teaching. In Hyltenstam and Pienemann.

Los Angeles County Office of Education, 1983. *Sheltered English: Content area instruction for limited English proficient students—training guide.* Los Angeles, CA: Los Angeles County Office of Education.

McCloskey, Mary Lou, Hooper, Susan and Linse, Caroline, 1991. *Teaching language, literature, and culture: A multicultural early childhood program.* Reading, MA: Addison-Wesley Publishing Company.

Mohan, Bernard A., 1986. *Language and content.* Reading, MA: Addison-Wesley Publishing Company.

Oller, John W., Jr., and Richard-Amato, Patricia A., Eds., 1983. *Methods that work.* Rowley, MA: Newbury House.

Penfield, Joyce, 1987. *The media: Catalysts for communicative language learning.* Reading, MA: Addison-Wesley Publishing Company.

Ramsey, P.,1987. *Teaching and learning in a diverse world: multicultural education for young children.* New York: Teacher's College Press.

Sage, Howard, 1987. *Incorporating literature in ESL instruction.* Englewood Cliffs, NJ: Prentice-Hall, Inc.

Savignon, Sandra J., 1988. *Communicative competence: Theory and classroom practice.* Reading, MA: Addison-Wesley Publishing Company.

Savignon, Sandra J., and Berns, Margie S., Eds., 1984. *Initiatives in communicative language teaching, Vol. I.* Reading, MA: Addison-Wesley Publishing Company.

Smallwood, Betty Ansin, 1991. *The literature connection: A read-aloud guide for multicultural classrooms.* Reading, MA: Addison-Wesley Publishing Company.

Smith, Stephen M., 1984. *The theater arts and the teaching of second languages.* Reading, MA: Addison-Wesley Publishing Company.

Terrell, Tracy D., 1983. The natural approach to language teaching: An update. In Oller and Richard-Amato.

Van Ek, J., 1975. *Systems development in adult language learning.* Strasbourg: Council of Europe.

Ventriglia, Linda, 1982. *Conversations of Miguel and Maria: How children learn a second language.* Reading, MA: Addison-Wesley Publishing Company.

Walker, Michael, 1992. *Addison-Wesley ESL.* Reading, MA: Addison-Wesley Publishing Company.

Wilkins, Beverly. Shared reading. *Elementary ESOL Education News,* Fall, 1984. Washington, DC: TESOL.

Wolf, D.P., 1989. "Portfolio assessment: Sampling student work," *Educational Leadership,* 46:7 pp. 35-39.